They Led

by Michael A. Ausel

Table of Contents

Consultant: John P. Boubel, Ph. D., History Professor
Bethany Lutheran College

It Takes a Leader

People are not always fair. They are not always kind. Sometimes it takes a special person—a leader—to show others what is right.

Elizabeth Blackwell
(1821-1910)

How did a shy little girl grow up to become the first woman doctor in the United States? Elizabeth Blackwell

may have been shy, but she believed in herself. Elizabeth kept writing letters to medical schools, hoping one would let her attend. Finally, after 29 tries, a medical school accepted her.

People long ago said that women's minds were too weak to study math and science. Elizabeth knew that was silly! She was the best student in her class. Still, Elizabeth had a hard time getting a job as a doctor.

Elizabeth opened her own hospital. She led the way and proved that women could be great doctors. Today, thousands of women doctors work all over the world helping people. Some even work in the hospital that Dr. Elizabeth Blackwell opened so long ago.

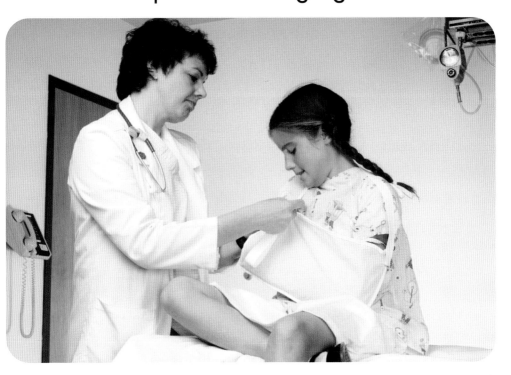

Cesar Chavez
(1927-1993)

When Cesar Chavez spoke, people listened. Cesar gave speeches in both English and Spanish. He spoke to farmworkers and college students. He spoke to big businesses, too. Cesar wanted everyone to understand that **unfair** ways had to change.

Cesar's family had been **migrant workers**. They traveled from farm to farm and home to home. They picked crops all day in the hot sun. Migrant workers were paid very little. If they asked for more pay or even a break to go to the bathroom, they could lose their jobs.

Cesar became a **union** leader. He led many workers in a **strike**. Thousands of workers marched with Cesar across California. They wanted everyone to know about their problems. At last, workers got more pay and better treatment. Cesar had led the way.

Helen Keller

(1880-1968)

Many people who are deaf use hand signs to "speak." When Helen Keller was little, she made up her own signs. It helped her family understand some of the things she needed. Helen had so much to say. She needed a better way to communicate.

Helen was blind as well as deaf. Many people said someone like Helen could not learn. Helen just needed the right teacher. Annie Sullivan taught Helen more signs. Then Helen learned to read **Braille**. Helen was able to study the subjects everyone else learned in school.

Later, Helen learned to place her fingertips on people's lips to "read" their words. She also learned to type. Helen became a famous writer. Her words **inspired** others to do their best and enjoy life just as she did.

Jackie Robinson
(1919-1972)

Once, not so long ago, African Americans could not work at the same jobs or live in the same neighborhoods where white people did. It took many brave Americans to change these unfair rules. One of these brave people was a baseball player named Jackie Robinson.

Jackie became a member of the Brooklyn Dodgers team in 1947. Before that, all the players on Major League Baseball teams had to be white. Some of the other players called Jackie names. He fought back, but not with his fists. He fought back by playing his best.

Because of Jackie, life in America changed both on and off the baseball field. He used his talents to lead the way to a better life for many people, just as Elizabeth Blackwell, Cesar Chavez, and Helen Keller had done.

Glossary

Braille   a special way of writing and printing created so that blind people can read with their fingers

inspire   to motivate people to do something

migrant workers   people who travel from place to place to do work

strike   when a group of workers stop doing their jobs until they get better pay or better working conditions

unfair   not fair or just

union   a group of workers who have joined together to ask for better pay and better working conditions

Index